Faith Focus

Adrian Taylor, Jr.

Unattributed quotations are by Adrian Taylor, Jr..

Unless otherwise indicated, Scripture quotations are from the King James Version of the Holy Bible.

All Hebrew and Greek translations are taken from the New Strong's Exhaustive Concordance of the Bible (Nashville, Tenn.: Thomas Nelson, Inc., 1995).

Published by Heard Word Publishing, LLC

Aurora, CO 80011

FAITH FOCUS VOLUME I

ISBN-13: 978-0-9801060-1-5

Copies of *Faith Focus Volume I* are available at www.ILikeChurch.org, www.TheGetOverItGal.com, and Amazon.com.

In honor of God, the Lord Jesus Christ, and the Holy Spirit, all references to their divinity and the Bible will be capitalized by choice of the publisher..

DEDICATION

I dedicate this book to my beloved wife, LaKenya Taylor, who has shown me undying loyalty and love. You, my love, have taught me by example what it means to have faith and stay focused. Thank you for being my wife. I love you.

CONTENTS

Acknowledgments   I

Introduction   Ii

1   There's No Such Thing as "Blind" Faith – Part 1   1

2   There's No Such Thing As "Blind" Faith – Part 2   5

3   Two Sides of Faith – Part 1   9

4   Two Sides of Faith – Part 2   12

5   Faith Working YOU   15

6   According to YOUR Faith – Part 1   18

7   According to YOUR Faith – Part 2   21

8   Don't Turn Back   25

9   Life In the Spirit   28

10   Keep Hope Alive   31

11   The Boldness to Believe   35

12   Maintaining Faith Even in Tragedy   38

13   Believing is Believing   42

14   Keys   45

15   Skillfulness   48

16   Look Again   51

17   It's Time To Eat!   55

18   Refocus   58

19   Why God Gave Us the Bible   62

20	Here's a 13 for You	65
21	Lessons From Enoch	68
22	No More Snackin'!	71
23	The Prayer Challenge	75
24	Uniting a House Divided	78
25	What are YOU Watching?	82
26	Dealing With Pressure	85
27	Just Know That You WIN!	89
28	You Are NOT Dead!	93
29	By-Products of Faith	96
30	Live and Have Peace	99
	Author's Bio	105

ACKNOWLEDGMENTS

I would like to thank my Spiritual Father, Apostle Maurice K Wright. Thank you for being an unending source of encouragement to my family and me.

I want to say thank you to my Mother, Deborah D. Taylor: you never let me be weak, and I am so grateful for that.

Thank you to the Lighthouse Church Family both in Denver & Cape Girardeau. You have sacrificed so much for me and my family and I am so humbled by your dedication and love. I love you all so much and I am glad that you allow me to lead you.

To my only begotten son, Joshua Taylor: I love you. Your compassionate and thoughtful heart has brought joy and peace to so many people. You inspire me to be a better man. I am so proud of you, Son. Stay humble and focused.

Lastly, I want to thank Beatrice Bruno for the way you have stood by me and pushed me to follow God. I would not be doing anything I am doing today without you. I had wanted to quit so much; but, your love and support strengthened me. Thank you for being a friend and now publisher. I love you and your family.

INTRODUCTION

Romans 10:17 (KJV)

So then faith cometh by hearing, and hearing by the word of God.

Hebrews 11:1 (KJV)

Now faith is the substance of things hoped for, the evidence of things not seen.

One must have faith in order to make God happy. That seems harsh, but the Lord is not unfair; He is righteous! He provides us with what we need to keep us abundantly supplied with faith. All we have to do is hear God's Word (the Bible) and faith shows up in our hearts empowering us to do His will.

This book is a compilation of a year's collection, of e-mails entitled *Friday Faith Focus*. These e-mails have been an encouragement to many people around the world, and are now available to you in the form of a devotional journal.

As you read these pages, there are questions to challenge you and space provided for your personal notes. Use this book during your prayer and meditation times to reflect and chart your spiritual development.

FAITH FOCUS #1

There's no such thing as "Blind" Faith

Part 1

--Sight Beyond Sight!--

I will never forget the lady who said to me, "It is just soooo hard to live by faith."

Although a very sweet lady, she was also a very sad lady. No matter how much I attempted to persuade her, she would not change her perspective. It was like throwing buckets of water on a brick wall; the wall gets wet but is unaffected. It remains hard and unchanged. Tragically, although this lady was precious and kind, she was unable to trust in God.

2 Corinthians5:7 (KJV)
For we walk by faith, not by sight.

The *first principle of faith* is contained in the above verse. Faith has nothing to do with what we see. The word "sight" means: the appearance, fashion, or shape. More specifically, sight refers to how we view a thing or situation.

If we choose to believe or not believe God based on what we see naturally, we are not walking in faith. Many of us fail to realize that because we are so affected by what we see, we are not people of faith.

God does not need favorable conditions to do miraculous things. This is important to know because faith should never be in men but in God. So, I don't need a sunny day or all my bills paid to trust God. These are all things I can see. These things do not change God's ability.

God can bake a delicious cake without any ingredients. He can make rain with no clouds in sight. Men need favorable conditions to work. But God, of and by Himself, can work well regardless of conditions.

Romans 10:17 (KJV)
...So then faith cometh by hearing, and hearing by the word of God.

This verse reveals the **second principle of faith**. Faith comes when I **hear** the Word of God. By combining these first two principles, I gain a real understanding that demystifies faith.

Praise Jesus!

We *need* faith to be simplified. If the lady I referenced earlier could grasp this understanding, she may think differently about faith.

As Christians, we need to understand that we must cease living by what we see. We need to embrace living by what we *hear* in God's Word (the Bible). That means we train ourselves to only be affected by what the Bible says.

If natural disaster comes, we remain strong in faith by resting in the truth that God is a *very present help in the time of trouble* (Psalms 46:1.)

If the doctor provides us with a bad diagnosis, we remain confident in faith by resting in the promise that Jesus' *stripes* have already healed us (1 Peter 2: 24.) We re-train ourselves to live according to the scriptures.

The Bible teaches us who God is, what He wants, and what He will do. As His children, we are obligated to please Him because we were *created for His pleasure* (Rev 4:11.)

However, it is *impossible* to put a smile on God's face if we have no faith (Hebrews 11:6.) Proper faith perspective is provided to us in the Bible - The Word of God!

Therefore, if we want to overcome any problem in this world and walk in the true blessing of God, we must familiarize ourselves with the Bible. Then, we can and will have faith and please God.

Reflections for Faith Focus #1

1. What is the first principle of faith?

2. What is the second principle of faith?

3. Take a moment and write what this Faith Focus means to you:

_____

_____

_____

_____

_____.

FAITH FOCUS #2

There's no such thing as "Blind" Faith

Part 2

–Sight Beyond Sight!–

Let me reiterate: **there is no such thing as blind faith!**

Actually, faith is the only way to truly *see* anything. Anyone who has a perspective other than God's is blind to the truth.

What is truth? St. John 17:17 clearly states that God's *Word is truth*. In Romans 10:17, we also see that God's Word is the conduit of faith. There is no faith without the Word of God (the Bible).

2 Cor. 5:7 (KJV)
For we walk by faith, not by sight...

Things you see with your eyes or experience in life can and will deceive you. As Christians, we are instructed not to focus on earthly things or be troubled by bad news. We have been given another way to see: faith!

When we hear about the economy, we can either become saddened and angered, or, we can find peace in God's promises. If we find ourselves in a huge financial bind, whether we caused it or not, God will make a way for us to fix it. How can we be certain of this? By faithfully studying and believing the Bible.

The promises in the Bible bring peace. If we obey God's Word, the hope we receive from that peace becomes reality. So then, faith from the Word becomes our illumination. We can see clearly because the Bible has given us hope to rely on what our natural eyes cannot detect.

I feel deeply sorry for anyone who is trapped by the limitations of this world. God is so much greater than what we can see!

John 4:24 (KJV)
God is a Spirit: and they that worship Him must worship Him in spirit and in truth.

Because God is a Spirit, He cannot be detected naturally. Nature serves as proof that God exists. Although it does not reveal Him or His will: it testifies to His supremacy.

How, then, do we connect to God? We connect to Him by and through faith. In other words, we believe the Bible for It is God's own testimony of Himself and His Will. He speaks to us and reveals Himself through His Word. No man conceived the scriptures; God spoke them to holy men by His Spirit!

Everything God wants us to know is revealed to us in the Bible. Who God is can be found in the Bible.

He tells Moses in Exodus 6 that He is Jehovah - the Self existent God. This indicates that God was not made or created; He exists of and by Himself. No one is greater than He.

In 1 Timothy 2, we see that God wants all men to be saved and come into the knowledge of the truth. He *expects* us to accept Christ and grow spiritually. To reject this is to reject the Will of God.

Family life, money, relationships, and how to overcome hard times are all revealed to us in the Bible. The way God wants us to live is conspicuously placed throughout the 66 books of the Old and New Testaments. As you read through the pages of the Bible, your eyes become open to God's truth about all things.

You may be surrounded in darkness, but Genesis Chapter 1 shows us that the Holy Spirit is present even in darkness. Therefore, your perception of darkness must change. You no longer have to be afraid of the dark because the Holy Spirit is there! That's worth shouting over! **Hallelujah**!

Study the Bible, friends. Until you do, your eyes will never be opened to God's true Will for your life.

Reflections for Faith Focus # 2

1. Why can't God be detected naturally?

2. How does the hope we receive from the Word of God become a reality?

3. Take a moment and write down what this Faith Focus has helped you realize.

_____

_____

_____

_____

_____

_____.

FAITH FOCUS #3

Two Sides of Faith

Part 1

Faith has been down-played by the world as some sort of religious group. People say things like, "I'm of the Catholic Faith." Or someone may ask, "Are you of the Islamic faith?"

Catholicism is a Denomination, and Islam is a World Religion. Neither of these groups are faith. Faith also has been associated with a strong emotion or feeling.

Again, someone might say, "I have faith that Johnny will do well on his exam."

This is a trap by the devil to keep us locked in the flesh. Emotionalism and feelings, as pure as they may seem, can never be faith. Our enemy, the devil, has labored long to remove the significance of faith in our society.

Hebrews 11:1 (KJV)

Now faith is the substance of things hoped for, the evidence of things not seen.

Romans 10:17 (KJV)

So then faith cometh by hearing, and hearing by the word of God.

Nowhere in the above verses do we read anything about religion or denomination. Faith is an unseen power which comes by the *hearing* of the Word of God. And the Word of God is the Bible.

You know how it is when you hear a good sermon or read a good scripture; you get energized. You feel like you can do anything!

That boost of encouragement is faith. It is the invisible divine enablement from God to those who will hear and obey Him. But, it comes by *hearing* the Word. Hearing is the first side of the **faith coin**. Therefore, if we do not have the Word of God, we don't have faith.

Mark 7:13 (KJV)
Making the word of God of none effect through your tradition, which ye have delivered: and many such like things do ye.

It is vital that we understand the importance of *hearing* the Word of God as it pertains to faith. Faith and the Word are related.

In the same manner a father produces a son through the mother, the Word of God produces faith in and through the hearer. So if the Word becomes ineffective, faith cannot exist. Then as stated in the above verse, tradition makes the Word of God non-effective.

Many religious and denominational traditions have voided the scriptures producing many fruitless people. A person can read the bible, go to church, even join a church or group. But, none of these actions means that one has faith. A person must be part of a church or group that shares the Word of God in righteousness. Then, that person must *hear* the Word of God clearly and grow in faith!

Reflections for Faith Focus # 3

1. Is faith a religion?

2. What is faith?

3. Why is the Word of God vital to faith?

4. Take a moment and write what this Faith Focus means to you:

_____

_____

_____

_____

_____.

FAITH FOCUS #4

Two Sides of Faith

Part 2

Last week I spoke very briefly about the "faith coin." Hearing is one side of that coin. Now, as we all know, a one-sided quarter is worthless; you cannot buy anything with it. Such a coin is considered *counterfeit*, and *counterfeiters are criminals*.

Oh yeah! You already know where I am going this week.

James 1:22 (KJV)

But be ye doers of the word, and not hearers only, deceiving your own selves.

If hearing the Word is only one side of the faith coin, and all I do is *hear* the Word, then I have a counterfeit faith. Many people are satisfied with just hearing the Word over and over and over and over. They enjoy telling and retelling stories of what God has said and done. Though that is great, it is deception if that is the totality of their Christian experience.

It is time we flip that coin over and see what should be on the other side. *Doing*, or *obeying*, is the other side of the faith coin.

James 2:26 (KJV)

For as the body without the spirit is dead, so faith without works is dead also.

Romans 10:17

Faith comes by hearing ...

FAITH FOCUS, VOLUME I

By *hearing*, we obtain faith. However, that faith will soon die if we don't put works with it. As a one-sided coin is useless, so also is faith without works.

In other words, we must *do* what God says just as willingly as we are to *hear* what God says. Hearing alone puts us in the worst category of deception: self- deception. The above verses clearly state that if all we do is hear and not obey, we deceive ourselves.

Putting works with our faith is the ultimate testament to one's love for and trust in God. James 2 shows us how Abraham, the father of the faith, demonstrated his faith by willingly obeying what he heard God tell him to do.

Side one: Abraham hears God speak. Faith comes when God tells him to sacrifice his son. Side two: Abraham obeys, or does, what God said. The faith he received when he *heard* the Lord came alive when he took his son up to the mountain top.

From that two-sided coin, Abraham cashed in on a powerful experience that not only taught him that God will provide, it taught his son also.

God revealed Himself there on that mountain as Jehovah Jireh - The Lord God, The Self-Existent God Who provides in and of Himself! He needs no one or no "thing" to provide for us. We just need to stop giving God counterfeit faith.

Come out of the deception of thinking you have something when you have nothing! Turn your nothing into something glorious by obeying the Lord! Make sure your faith has two sides.

Reflections for Faith Focus # 4

1. How can a person have counterfeit faith?

2. How does faith die?

3. What did Abraham & Isaac learn about God?

4. Take a moment and write what this Faith Focus means to you:

_____

_____

_____

_____

_____

_____.

FAITH FOCUS #5

Faith Working YOU

Like me, you may often ask yourself, *Why does it take so long for my faith to work?*

After much thought in regards to this question, I came to a most intriguing conclusion. Unfortunately, many people are only interested in what faith can do for them. But faith doesn't really work until *it* works *you*.

Acts 15:9 (KJV)
And put no difference between us and them, purifying their hearts by faith.

Faith purifies; if you let it. As we all know, faith comes by *hearing* the Word of God. The more we *hear* it, the more our faith is reinforced. The problem, though, is that faith causes us to go through some much needed changes in order to experience the promises of God.

James 1:3 (KJV)
Knowing this, that the trying of your faith worketh patience.

Because of all the challenges to faith - time, people, circumstances, fear - faith first starts to work into us other spiritual elements we need to successfully live by faith. Faith builds patience! There is only one way to build patience: **wait**.

Oh Lord, help us all!

Isaiah 40:31 (KJV)
But they that wait upon the Lord shall renew their strength; they shall mount up with wings as eagles; they

shall run, and not be weary; and they shall walk, and not faint.

Look at that: faith *builds* patience. This means we have to *wait* on God. When we submit to God by waiting on and serving Him, we receive renewed strength, supernatural power, and endurance. This is one of the key principles we need that will help us to understand the process of faith. Faith not only works *for* us, it works something greater *in* us as well.

Hebrews 6:12 (KJV)
That ye be not slothful, but followers of them who through faith and patience inherit the promises.

The above verse instructs us to not be slothful. Instead, Hebrews 6:12 encourages us to follow after those who, through faith **and** patience, inherit (or obtain) the promises of God. If faith had a twin brother, his name would be "patience" because they work together.

The *faith* comes from God: He provides that through His Word. The *patience* comes from us *if* we submit to God and obey His Word.

So, when you wonder why faith isn't working, ask yourself if you are letting faith work you.

Reflections for Faith Focus # 5

1. What happens to faith the more you hear it?

2. Faith builds what?

3. What happens when you submit to serving & waiting on God?

4. Take a moment and write what this Faith Focus means to you:

_____

_____

_____

_____

_____.

FAITH FOCUS #6

According to YOUR Faith

Part 1

Matthew 9:27-29 (KJV)

And when Jesus departed thence, two blind men followed Him, crying, and saying, Thou Son of David, have mercy on us. [28] And when He was come into the house, the blind men came to Him: and Jesus saith unto them, Believe ye that I am able to do this? They said unto Him, Yea, Lord. [29] Then touched He their eyes, saying, According to your faith be it unto you.

One of the reasons I love this passage is because it plainly shows how God deals with children differently. Some think this is unfair, but, we all do this.

A baby is not treated the same as a five-year old. Nor is a teenager treated the same as a nine-year old. God is the best Father, and He knows all of His kids. Therefore, He specializes in dealing with each of us.

In the above passage, Jesus is approached by two blind men who address Him as the Son of David. This is of note because it means that, although they were blind, they understood their covenant rights.

Sometimes, we are blinded by the troubles of this life. We must never lose sight of God's promises no matter how dark things get!

These men cried for the Lord's mercy. Jesus saw a greater need and redirected their focus. They didn't need God's mercy; they needed to believe.

You see, as we grow in God, we must work *with* Him. We can't just cry for help and think everything is left up to God. He expects us to walk in faith. In other words: **believe**!

Mark 9:23 (KJV)
Jesus said unto him, If thou canst believe, ALL things are possible to him that believeth.

Look at what Jesus said: there are **no** limitations to the ones who *actively* believe. This is why we must grow spiritually: so we can become skillful in learning how to believe and trust in God totally! Then, and only then, are we proven faithful enough to handle the true inheritance the Lord has in store for us.

Those two blind men wanted their sight. Unfortunately, they held on to an infantile perspective. Jesus, desiring to encourage their growth, asked if they believed. When they replied yes, Jesus challenged them further by leaving their healing up to their level of faith.

In a sense, they wanted to be picked up and carried. Instead, Jesus held out His arms and made them walk to Him.

So, if you are pleading with God to do something and He seems to be ignoring you, chances are He is waiting for you to exercise your faith. In other words, stop crying and walk to Him!

Reflections for Faith Focus # 6

1. God is the best Father because He knows all of His what?

2. Never lose sight of God's what?

3. God will often redirect us from mercy to what?

4. Take a moment and write what this Faith Focus means to you:

_____

_____

_____

_____

_____

_____.

FAITH FOCUS #7

According to YOUR Faith

Part 2

Matthew 9:27-29 (KJV)

And when Jesus departed thence, two blind men followed Him, crying, and saying, Thou Son of David, have mercy on us. [28] And when He was come into the house, the blind men came to Him: and Jesus saith unto them, Believe ye that I am able to do this? They said unto Him, Yea, Lord. [29] Then touched He their eyes, saying, According to your faith be it unto you.

Jesus makes a beautiful statement: *According to your faith.*

The word 'accord' means to be in agreement with something. It lends to references about harmony.

In music, a basic triad is three distinct notes played together to form a harmonious chord. The C major chord is formed by three notes: C, E, & G. They are individual notes with clear sounds. When played together, they are in accord. They agree. They are harmonious.

You don't have to be a classically trained musician to determine if notes harmonize; the sound tells it all. Notes are individual; but, if you play two bad notes together, everyone knows it.

This is a perfect example for our faith walk. Faith is like a note with a distinct sound; we give off a sound as well. The question then becomes, do we produce a sound that harmonizes with the faith God gave us? Are we and faith in accord?

Matthew 15:8 (KJV)

This people draweth nigh unto Me with their mouth, and honoureth Me with their lips; but their heart is far from Me.

This is a prime example of disunity! Examine yourself closely now. Jesus says that there is a people, who honor Him with their lips, but their heart is far from Him. They say,

"Oh, I trust God!" "He is able!" "The Lord is Worthy!"

However, in their heart, they have no respect for the Lord. Their heart leads them to say and do things that dishonor God. They are not in accord with faith. They speak faith but live something entirely different. This is not harmony with the Spirit of God.

Proverbs 23:7 (KJV)

For as he thinketh in his heart, so is he: Eat and drink, saith he to thee; but his heart is not with thee.

Jeremiah 17:9 (KJV)

The heart is deceitful above all things, and desperately wicked: who can know it?

Matthew 12:34 (KJV)

O generation of vipers, how can ye, being evil, speak good things? for out of the abundance of the heart the mouth speaketh.

I know this is a lot of scripture, but it is imperative that we grow in the truth. And the truth, according to John 17:17, is the Word of God. The heart reveals the true character and nature of a person and the mouth reveals what's in the heart. Jesus, however, goes further than words. He wants more than lip service. He wants faith.

Luke 18:8 (KJV)

I tell you that He will avenge them speedily. Nevertheless when the Son of man cometh, shall He find faith on the earth?

James 2:26 (KJV)

For as the body without the spirit is dead, so faith without works is dead also.

Jesus looks for faith! He always finds a way to pull faith out of people. Regardless of whether it was the woman with the issue of blood or the man with the withered hand, Jesus always brought out at least an ounce of faith in people. He **made** them harmonize with Him.

Jesus is like a piano tuner; He tweaks us until we resonate with the right sound. Neither crying, nor whining, nor complaining produces the right sound that He attempts to evoke from us.

Now, Jesus will work on us - and that is not always comfortable - until He hears His Word flow from us and sees our obedience to Him. This is the sound He is searching for.

Our goal is to live in agreement with God. We must seek to honor the Lord with more than our mouths. Our lives and actions should harmonize with God.

So, beware of fear and pride. They are contaminates to God's will for our lives. No matter how hard things get in this economy or in our lives, keep harmonizing with faith. God is going to provide for you regardless of the economy. Fear not... Only believe!

Reflections for Faith Focus # 7

1. What does the word 'accord' mean?

2. What is truth?

3. What is our goal?

4. Take a moment and write what this Faith Focus means to you:

_____

_____

_____

_____

_____.

FAITH FOCUS #8

Don't Turn Back

Lift up your hands and shout, "I will not turn back!"

Go ahead... do it now. Whether you are at work or at home with your feet up, declare now that you will not turn back!

Hebrews 10:38-39 (KJV)

Now the just shall live by faith: but if any man draw back, My soul shall have no pleasure in him. [39] But we are not of them who draw back unto perdition; but of them that believe to the saving of the soul.

Faith requires tenacity and endurance. Numerous people turn back because they are deceived into thinking the spiritual life is easy. You don't just yell at the devil, shout at church, and then everything will be happily ever after!

The Bible is not a fairy tale. It is a strategic battle plan for living this life and glorifying God. You can be certain of this one thing: God is not glorified by anyone who turns back.

The scripture clearly illuminates that the just (The Born Again Christian Believer) shall live by faith. It also reveals that if anyone draws back, God has no pleasure in that person. Anyone who draws back from faith ceases from pleasing God and enters into a place of damnable destruction.

Perdition means damnable destruction. In fact, perdition also means loss, waste, or ruin. To be more precise, perdition means to perish or to die. To live any way other than by faith is like driving full speed towards a cliff; death is inevitable.

Matthew 7:13-14 (KJV)

Enter ye in at the strait gate: for wide is the gate, and

*broad is the way, that leadeth to destruction, and many
there be which go in thereat: [14] Because strait is the
gate, and narrow is the way, which leadeth unto life, and
few there be that find it.*

Again, the easy way doesn't exist. Faith is challenging, but
it leads to life. The easy way is wide and heavily populated; it
ends in the mass murder of all who walk its path. I urge you
with all that is in me...PLEASE DO NOT TURN BACK!

No matter what tragedy has occurred, stay focused on
Christ. Many good Christian people started off in righteousness;
then, something happened that impeded their progress. Don't
allow rape, death, or loss to turn you away to destruction.

Divorce is bad, but you can overcome that by faith. You may
have lost a job, but you can overcome that as well. Stay focused!
It may be tough, but you're pleasing God. Turning away only
pleases you.

Too many have turned away. Lot's wife turned away and
died. Orpah turned away from Naomi and Ruth and was never
heard of again. Judas turned away and the devil entered him.

The good news, though, for any of you who have turned
away is that you still have time to turn back and embrace the
Lord again. Peter turned away but Jesus restored him.

Reflections for Faith Focus # 8

1. Faith requires what & what?

2. The Bible is not a fairy tale, it is a what?

3. The easy way doesn't what?

4. Take a moment and write what this Faith Focus means to you:

_____

_____

_____

_____

_____.

FAITH FOCUS #9

Life in the Spirit

We have all heard it said, *without faith it is impossible to please* God. With so many people abandoning faith, I wonder: does anybody still desire to please the Lord?

I mean, if I want to please God, faith must be the key element utilized to accomplish my goal of pleasing Him. That makes sense to me. But, there are so many people today who want God to ignore His Word and be happy with their misery. I can assure you, friend: God does not enjoy your misery.

John 4:24 (KJV)
God is a Spirit: and they that worship Him must worship Him in spirit and in truth.

John 6:63 (KJV)
It is the spirit that quickeneth; the flesh profiteth nothing: the words that I speak unto you, they are spirit, and they are life.

God is a Spirit! He cannot be seen or detected with any natural instrument or tool. In order to relate to Him, we must receive and believe His Word, which is also Spirit.

Since the Spirit quickens or gives life, it behooves us to always acknowledge the supremacy of the Spirit over natural things. God is greatly blessed when we focus on Him and not on what we can see. There is no greater honor for the Lord!

God knows it is a challenge for us to ignore the world around us and our personal experiences to trust in Him. That is why He is pleased when we walk in faith. It is a huge sacrifice to believe God. When we do, however, we receive life. Focusing on

God gives us hope and renewed strength, two of the benefits of faith. Our faith reinforces us so we can endure.

There is not much hope in watching the world. Just a glimpse at CNN can cause depression. Declining markets and international hostility can create much fear. Watching God helps us understand that no matter how difficult things become, the Lord will see us through victoriously!

God always gives us what we need in order to do what He wants us to do. He wants us to walk by faith because He is pleased by our faith walk. To assist and guide us, He has made His Word available to us. His Word, then, provides us with life so we can overcome every obstacle.

The main reason people are so tired and weary is because they are trying to live outside of faith and the Word of God. They have no life because they are outside of the Spirit.

.

So live by faith according to the Word of God. Faith is your power source. Live to please God. It may be a struggle at times, but you **will** overcome every challenge.

Reflections for Faith Focus # 9

1. Faith is the key element to what?

2. God cannot be seen or detected by what?

3. What has God provided us with to please Him?

4. Take a moment and write what this Faith Focus means to you:

_____

_____

_____

_____

_____

FAITH FOCUS #10

Keep Hope Alive

As long as we have hope, our faith has a job. Where there is no more hope, faith is now unemployed. A lack of hope removes us from God's planned best for our lives. Oh yes! God has planned so much good for us, and He makes it happen in our lives through faith.

In other words, it is undetected by any natural instrument. This goodness is only available to us as we trust God by yielding to His will and obeying His Word.

Jeremiah 29:11 (KJV)
For I know the thoughts that I think toward you, saith the Lord, thoughts of peace, and not of evil, to give you an expected end.

Now we all know this verse. Most of us can quote it by heart. But, quoting it by heart is no good if we don't believe it. This verse reveals to us God's true intentions and thoughts concerning us.

The main purpose of the Bible is to reveal and give hope to us for what we cannot see. If we lose sight of this purpose by believing what we see and experience every day, then we kill our hope.

We have to be fully persuaded that God's plan for our lives is good and peaceful. Once we are settled in that truth, we have to remain hopeful; no matter what. How do we do that? I am glad you asked.

We must remain faithful and diligent to obey God. Let nothing make us inconsistent in the Lord. By this, we prove our love to God and sow seeds of righteousness. As we faithfully praise and serve the Lord, He strengthens us with joy and grace.

Praise God!

We can always tell when someone has lost hope – his or her conversation is no longer of faith. Instead, the person's conversation is of giving up. He or she sounds as though death has come and there is no life within. This person has accepted the lie that things will just be as they are. Their hope has long died. They are blinded to the glorious promises of God's wondrous provisions.

A people who hope are vibrant! They are filled with joyous expectation. Everything in their life can be in total disarray and chaos; you would never know it because they speak of their expectation in the Lord.

Yes! Things are hard for them, but their mind is too focused on Jesus to be worried about their petty challenges. Even life-threatening situations cannot force them to blaspheme the integrity and greatness of God!

Proverbs 14:14 (KJV)
The backslider in heart shall be filled with his own ways: and a good man shall be satisfied from himself.

Saints, we cannot afford to be backsliders in our heart. Most people think of backsliders as people who commit vile sins of adultery or drug addiction. Tragically, it is possible to claim Christ and be in a backslidden condition.

The above verse, says that a person who is full of his own ways is a backslider in his heart. Anytime we don't trust God and hope in His Word, we have turned away from God's way to devise our own way. That is a backslider.

The one who does not hope has fired his or her faith. Consequently, this person has just made it impossible to please God and has become a backslider in his or her heart. The only good thing about being a backslider is that God is still married to you. But what good is it to be married to Someone you are not committed to?

Reflections for Faith Focus # 10

1. When is faith unemployed?

2. What must you be fully persuaded of?

3. What is the sign of a people who hope?

4. Take a moment and write what this Faith Focus means to you:

_____

_____

_____

_____

_____

_____.

FAITH FOCUS #11

The Boldness to Believe

Mark 9:23-24 (KJV)

Jesus said unto him, If thou canst believe, all things are possible to him that believeth. [24] And straightway the father of the child cried out, and said with tears, Lord, I believe; help Thou mine unbelief.

I was talking with my mother yesterday morning as I rode to my office. It is quite common for us to talk about the Lord. As we discussed some personal things concerning our family, she made a statement about fear that sparked this week's exhortation.

She said, "Fear must be removed. If God is true, then we **must** believe."

I am always inspired by those around me. So today, my mother gets the credit for allowing the Holy Spirit to speak through her. To play on the old cliché: Thanks, Mom!

Yes, friends, we must recognize that fear hinder us from trusting in the Lord. God is not some slick, fast-talking guy trying to impress us with fancy words. When He speaks, the mountains tremble! The whole of creation awaits His Voice!

We cannot afford to treat God's Word as if It is simply a mundane verse or rhyme. His Word is not sent to cheer us up! His Word is our fuel to walk in the impossible!

When you put gasoline in your car, you don't wonder if it will drive. The gas is the fuel which propels the car so it can perform the way it was designed to function. You, my friend, were designed to perform supernaturally. Your fuel source is not food or water. The fuel that propels you is the Living Word of God: The Bible!

Mark 5:36 (KJV)

As soon as Jesus heard the word that was spoken, He saith unto the ruler of the synagogue, Be not afraid, only believe.

Oh, praise God! All things are possible to those who believe! Don't fear! Believe!

Jesus tells us to believe instead of fearing. So when fear arises, this is your cue to radically believe. All you have to do is be aware of what's going on around you. When fear shows up - and it will - start believing!

That's right! When fear comes, start believing. The man in Mark 9 showed us how to do it. He confessed that he *did* believe the Lord. Many of us do believe; fear just gets in the way.

You can beat fear by confessing to God. The man in Mark 9 also confessed he did fear, and he asked God to help him with unbelief. God will strengthen you to overcome fear if you are honest with Him.

2 Cor. 4:13 (KJV)

We having the same spirit of faith, according as it is written, I believed, and therefore have I spoken; we also believe, and therefore speak;

Once you overcome fear, keep speaking God's word. Speak what you believe. If you believe the Lord, speak it boldly. Do not speak death. Even if death is all around you, speak life. Believe, saints, because we are facing times which demand that we believe. The world needs the supernatural you. Focus on His Word and believe!

Reflections for Faith Focus # 11

1. What has fear come to do?

2. You were designed to perform how?

3. What should you do when fear comes?

4. Take a moment and write what this Faith Focus means to you:

_____

_____

_____

_____.

FAITH FOCUS #12

Maintaining Faith Even in Tragedy

Isaiah 61:3 (KJV)

To appoint unto them that mourn in Zion, to give unto them beauty for ashes, the oil of joy for mourning, the garment of praise for the spirit of heaviness; that they might be called trees of righteousness, the planting of the Lord, that He might be glorified.

I recently commemorated the 3-year anniversary of the birth and death of my daughter. I know the Golden Rule for preachers seems to be "never be vulnerable." However, I believe the best way to impact someone's life is to reveal your scars so others may know just how capable God is. Therefore, yesterday was a somewhat difficult time for my family and me.

I don't know if you have ever faced tragedy. When it comes, it often arrives without warning. I was certainly not prepared for it. Nobody expects to go into a delivery room and be handed a dead baby; but, that is what happened to me.

After being told that our daughter was not alive, my wife could not bring herself to even look at our beautiful baby and was rolled back to her room. I, on the other hand, stood in the middle of a now empty delivery room holding the lifeless body of the daughter I had so badly wanted for years. How do you move on in the face of such disaster?

2 Cor. 5:7 (KJV)

(For we walk by faith, not by sight:)

The devil would have you to believe that it is hard to move on or even lead a full life after tragedy strikes. That is a lie! The truth is simple: you move on by faith! The hard part is learning how to let go of what you have seen, felt, and experienced in order to embrace the Strength of the Lord.

In that moment, I had to find strength.

I have too much depending on me. I can't afford to be depressed. My wife needs me to pour strength into her. My son needs his dad to guide him through this. These are the things I told myself as I made the decision to rest in the Lord.

Isaiah 25:8 (KJV)
He will swallow up death in victory; and the Lord God will wipe away tears from off all faces; and the rebuke of His people shall He take away from off all the earth: for the Lord hath spoken it.

I went into the bathroom of my wife's hospital room and cried. I got on my knees and cried before the Lord. I did not ask God *"Why?"*That was irrelevant. I needed God to just tell me what to do. As I knelt on the floor of that bathroom, God spoke to me.

This is how I feel when men die and go to hell. But one day, you will see your daughter again, He told me.

At that moment, peace came upon me. Instantly, I knew what I had to do: I had to win souls to Christ!

No; God did not kill my baby to teach me this lesson. Satan thought he had crippled me. Instead, God drew close and fellowshipped with me. That was the beginning of my healing process.

The deception with tragedy is this; it makes you focus on yourself. It also impedes your doing what God designed you to do: minister to others. Does that mean you should not hurt or mourn? Real men cry! Women too! The Holy Spirit is our Comforter, but we never stay self-focused.

I focused on Christ instead of myself. I surrendered to God and rested in Him. In doing so, I was able to fellowship with God and learn what touches His heart.

Philippians 3:10 (KJV)

That I may know Him, and the power of His resurrection, and the fellowship of His sufferings,..

When we suffer, the Lord is never far from us. In fact, He draws closer. If we look to Him instead of any other place, the Lord will reveal Himself to us in a new way. When I learned what touches His heart, it empowered me to be a better man, husband, father, pastor, and minister.

There isn't a day that goes by that I don't think about my daughter. Fortunately, even in weakness, I have learned how to grasp the Strength of God and beat back the spirit of depression. That is faith! Things may not go the way you want, but keep your faith. You may have lost someone or thing special, but do not lose your faith in God.

You are not weak because you suffer or go through great hardship; you are weak only if you let go of your faith and stop focusing on Christ. If you focus on Him, no matter what, you will have strength to overcome. Keep the faith!

Reflections for Faith Focus # 12

1. Where is the Lord when we suffer?

2. What is the deception of tragedy?

3. What does the devil want you to believe?

4. Take a moment and write what this Faith Focus means to you:

_____

_____

_____

_____

_____.

FAITH FOCUS #13

Believing is Believing

Hebrews 11:1 (KJV)

Now faith is the substance of things hoped for, the evidence of things not seen.

Do you realize that God is working on your behalf right now? You can't see it, but He is. This is the challenge of faith. It is based on our willingness to trust in what God **says** instead of what we can *see, touch,* or *experience*.

2 Cor. 5:19 (KJV)

To wit, that God was in Christ, reconciling the world unto Himself, not imputing their trespasses unto them; and hath committed unto us the word of reconciliation.

When Jesus walked the face of this planet, God was in Him working a plan of redemption. Yes! God worked while Jesus walked out His will. Nobody could *see* what God was doing. Even the religious leaders of His day were oblivious to God's plan. The devil certainly was blind to what God was doing through Christ!

You have to understand this - Jesus did not fit the mold. He looked nothing like what people wanted. He was not prominent. He was not educated. He came from Nazareth. Now I know He is your Lord and means a lot to you, but, 2000 years ago, Jesus was nobody!

God loves to use nobodies! He specializes in working great things through underdogs and wretches. This is why everyone was so astonished by Jesus; He looked like a regular guy. Inside, though, He was the Christ!

He was questioned constantly about His authority to say what He said. Nobody could **get** Him. Only those who were able to live beyond what they saw received of His blessing.

<u>Col. 1:27 (KJV)</u>

To whom God would make known what is the riches of the glory of this mystery among the Gentiles; which is Christ in you, the hope of glory:

Now, my friends, Christ is in you. God is in you also working His plan. You cannot see it, but you know that God has made some precious promises to you.

You may feel ordinary or insignificant; be like Jesus! Walk in obedience to God every day. Let nothing slow you down because Christ is in you, and He will soon reveal His glory through you.

Reflections for Faith Focus # 13

1. God loves to use who?

2. Why was everyone so astonished with Jesus?

3. Who is inside of you?

4. Take a moment and write what this Faith Focus means to you:

_____

_____

_____

_____

_____.

FAITH FOCUS #14

Keys

Matthew 16:19 (KJV)

And I will give unto thee the keys of the kingdom of heaven: and whatsoever thou shalt bind on earth shall be bound in heaven: and whatsoever thou shalt loose on earth shall be loosed in heaven.

Peter was afforded the keys to Jesus' house because he was able to tap into the right knowledge - the knowledge that Jesus is the Christ!

Yes, indeed! Many of us take this information for granted. But, this is the most important truth we could ever hope to realize: Jesus is the Christ He is not "A" Christ; He is "THE" Christ! He is *The One and Only Emissary of Salvation and Redemption Anointed with God's Ability and Authority.*

When Peter learned this truth, Jesus gave him unlimited access to Heaven. As a result of our common faith in Christ, we are all beneficiaries of this same promise; we get keys just like Peter.

This is beautiful! Anything we need has already been provided because of the keys. If you need healing, you have the keys. If you need peace, the keys are in your possession. If you need provision of any kind, use those keys. We can never blame God for anything because He has given us the keys to His house.

Now, keys, just like anything else, have to be utilized! You can't just hold a set of keys in your hand and complain. Even if a door is locked, it is powerless to prevent your advancement because you have the keys. Let us remember not to forget or misplace those keys. Without them, we lose access. Keep the knowledge of Christ at the forefront of your mind.

Rev. 1:18 (KJV)
I am He that liveth, and was dead; and, behold, I am alive for evermore, Amen; and have the keys of hell and of death.

If it seems as though you have misplaced your keys, don't worry: Jesus has a set of keys as well. Your keys give you access to heaven. His keys, however, control everything. So, when you are going through hell or feel close to death, remember: Jesus wields the power to restrain death and hell!

Reflections for Faith Focus # 14

1. How did Peter get the keys?

2. There's no reason to complain when you hold what in your hands?

3. Take a moment and write what this Faith Focus means to you:

_____

_____

_____

_____

_____.

FAITH FOCUS #15

Skillfulness

2 Cor. 5:7 (KJV)
(For we walk by faith, not by sight:)

Faith is not spooky! It is the disciplined, practical application of our obedience to God's Word. Yes! I just cussed at you by using the word *discipline*.

Unfortunately, many Christians are undisciplined and unskilled in the Word of Righteousness. Thank God that this is a changing dynamic!

Hebrews 5:13 (KJV)
For every one that useth milk is unskilful in the word of righteousness: for he is a babe.

What this particular verse of scripture means is that, if you use milk, you can't stand under instruction, correction, or constructive criticism. You blame others. You always have an excuse.

It is this writer's humble opinion that the worst trait of milk users is they are un-teachable. The Bible calls this type of person a "babe." A person is a babe because he or she is unskillful in the Word of God. This person doesn't know how to use the Bible to overcome and find victory. He or she wants victory but has no skills to achieve the desired outcome.

An unskilled Christian is like a kid on a little league basketball team. The coach lets everyone join the team; nobody gets cut. The bitter truth, however, is that if a particular child has no skills, he or she doesn't play very much in the game.

Knowing the rules or liking a sport will never substitute for skill. The same principle applies to the Word of God: we have to do more than just memorize scriptures.

Becoming skillful in the Bible is much like becoming proficient at anything; it requires knowledge and discipline. We must train ourselves to focus only on truth: the Word of God. Speak only what God says. Resist the temptation of fear, and determine never to quit.

You cannot just know what to do; you must *do* what you know to do. Only then are you truly walking by faith. It's not spooky. It is simple. Hear God and obey Him.

I will leave you with this: skillful means experienced. Many are not skillful because they have never truly applied the Word of God to their experiences and stood on It. I know I haven't always done it. You don't gain experience by having a job; you gain experience by doing a job well. Now go do it in the name of Jesus!

Reflections for Faith Focus # 15

1. What is the worst thing about a milk user?

2. Biblical skillfulness requires knowledge & what?

3. Why are many not skillful?

4. Take a moment and write what this Faith Focus means to you:

_____

_____

_____

_____

_____.

FAITH FOCUS #16

Look Again

<u>1 Kings 18:41-44 (KJV)</u>

And Elijah said unto Ahab, Get thee up, eat and drink; for there is a sound of abundance of rain. [42] So Ahab went up to eat and to drink. And Elijah went up to the top of Carmel; and he cast himself down upon the earth, and put his face between his knees, [43] And said to his servant, Go up now, look toward the sea. And he went up, and looked, and said, There is nothing. And he said, Go again seven times. [44] And it came to pass at the seventh time, that he said, Behold, there ariseth a little cloud out of the sea, like a man's hand. And he said, Go up, say unto Ahab, Prepare thy chariot, and get thee down, that the rain stop thee not.

God is faithful! Oh yes; God is FAITHFUL! That is not just a saying; it is the truth!

Sadly, though, some of us only say it with our mouths because we have lost the passion to actively believe God. In our hearts, we secretly hide the disappointment of failed expectations. But, we know better than to let go of God entirely! We get tired, even exhausted, with not seeing what we know God has promised; so we settle into a pattern of complacency.

Trying to protect our hearts from more traumas, we go through the motions of Christianity. We step back from responsibility and service to the Lord. We become less faithful and occupy our time pleasing our flesh since we can't seem to be satisfied through our faith the way we would like. We know enough to stay close to God because we know He can do anything, and, on the off chance He decides to supernaturally move in our lives, we leave the back door open.

Leaving the back door of our lives open to God, though, is a problem. This is deception. In trying to protect ourselves from hurt expectations, we end up cutting ourselves deeper.

This is like a person who does not like a pungent odor in the air. By locking himself inside an air-tight room, he may not be able to smell the unpleasant fragrance any longer. However, the room he is in will soon run out of air. He is not dead yet, but he will be very soon. He has cut himself off from his source of life just because he could not stand the smell around him.

Believing and trusting God does not always smell or feel good, but we never cut ourselves off. We continue to believe because we know that God cannot lie. He has made a promise to us.

The Prophet Elijah was under great pressure. However, he never let what he did not see stop him from believing; he *knew* God was faithful. Elijah was convinced of what God shared with him. God revealed to him that an abundant rain was coming; Elijah told the King even though there was no sign that rain was coming. He told his servant to go look for it. His servant brought back a negative report; Elijah told him to look again. Still the servant returned with bad news.

Again, the man of God would not submit to failed expectations. He told his servant to go back and look again. All the while, Elijah was birthing, through prayer, what God had placed in his spirit. His head was between his legs. This is the same position doctors place women in when they are ready to birth a child. Elijah pushed, through prayer, while he waited for a confirmation of his faith.

Again, his servant returned with nothing but disappointment. I am certain that, although his faith was shaken, Elijah was more convinced than ever of God's truth. Undisturbed by what he saw, Elijah prayed more and sent his servant out again. Elijah's example testifies that the only way to overcome fear and disappointment is to hit harder and strengthen your faith through prayer and active believing.

Elijah shows us how *not* to give in to the frustration: hit harder! Seven times he sends his servant out, and on the seventh, the servant returns with news of a small cloud. That little cloud grew and filled the sky to saturate the ground with rain. God fulfilled His promise to Elijah because Elijah would not stop actively believing. He birthed rain through faith!

As we move forward, remember: **God is faithful!** This is a year for birthing; be prepared to labor to bring forth the promises of God.

For those of you who have grown weary from bad and negative news, be encouraged! Take a posture of prayer and look again. Not just once, though. Keep looking until the promise is revealed. Don't give up; look again! If you see nothing, look again. It is guaranteed that you will eventually look up and see what you know God has shared with you!

Reflections for Faith Focus # 16

1. Why do we go through the motions of Christianity?

2. Why is it important to keep believing?

3. Why was God able to fulfill His promise to Elijah?

4. Take a moment and write what this Faith Focus means to you:

_____

_____

_____

_____

_____.

FAITH FOCUS #17

It's Time to Eat!

Psalm 23:4-5 (KJV)

Yea, though I walk through the valley of the shadow of death, I will fear no evil: for thou art with me; thy rod and thy staff they comfort me. [5] Thou preparest a table before me in the presence of mine enemies: thou anointest my head with oil; my cup runneth over.

Just the sign of hardship makes some folks quake in their boots! But, since we walk by faith and not by sight, hardship means something completely different to us.

When enemies show their ugly heads, we rejoice! Why? Because they represent an unequivocal symbol: they serve to remind us that *it is time to eat!*

That's right! God loves an audience when He works. His audience of choice is filled with all your enemies.

Every person who says you are hopeless and can't make it is your enemy. People who plot your demise are your enemies. The hard and difficult times you face as you press to believe God are enemies as well. Needless to say, then, you already know the devil is your enemy, too!

These are your enemies because they have one thing in common; they serve to remove you from your faith in God. This is why you have to fight for your faith.

Don't worry, though; when enemies appear, rejoice! If two or three show up, shout louder! And if more come, give God a crazy praise! The more the merrier!

The appearance of enemies is a sign of blessing: God is about to serve you the meal He has promised. This is wonderful! He prepares a table before you in the *presence* of your enemies.

We all want the anointing and the overflow, but God has planned to bless you in front of the devil. So send out invitations to all your enemies. Keep a mailing list so you can invite them to the feast. When you see the devil and things are getting rough, shout loud and take out your fork because **it is time to eat!**

Reflections for Faith Focus # 17

1. What do enemies serve to remind us of?

2. List some characteristics of enemies?

3. The appearance of enemies is a sign of what?

4. Take a moment and write what this Faith Focus means to you:

_____

_____

_____

_____

_____.

FAITH FOCUS #18

Refocus

<u>Jeremiah 9:23-24 (KJV)</u>
Thus saith the Lord, Let not the wise man glory in his wisdom, neither let the mighty man glory in his might, let not the rich man glory in his riches: [24] But let him that glorieth glory in this, that he understandeth and knoweth Me, that I am the Lord which exercise lovingkindness, judgment, and righteousness, in the earth: for in these things I delight, saith the Lord.

Several years ago, a man committed suicide because he lost a considerable amount of money. News reports indicated that he had nearly 17 billion dollars: that's **$17,000,000,000.00**. As the economy sloped further downward, he lost 8 **billion** dollars leaving him with a mere 9 **billion** dollars! As we all know, in these harsh economic times, no one can *possibly* live on **9 billion dollars**! So, he killed himself!

Life is far more than riches; it is a gift from God. Tragically, too many of us use our lifetime on the earth as a time for personal gain and pursuits. As a result, such as in the previous paragraph, when we lose things, we diminish the value and purpose of our own lives. Therefore, it is easy for someone whose focus is other than God to take his or her own life: they lose sight of their true purpose for living.

If getting a big house is my reason for living and I never get it, I will never experience peace or feel accomplished in life. If I do get that big house and somehow lose it, I feel like a failure. Even worse, if I get the house and keep it, my life somehow finds meaning because I have a big house. The house is my god; it defines me. It is my source of joy and peace. If it goes, so does my reason for living.

People all over the world have the wrong focus. Many of you reading this today, as wonderful as you are, have the wrong focus. You have no peace. You are sick. You stress out over unimportant stuff. Why? Because someone told you that you have to have a lot of stuff in order to be respected. The only thing you **need** is to know God.

In this life, you will experience good days and bad days. Knowing God is the only reason we are still here today. Excuse me a moment while I digress.

Jeremiah reveals to us that pride sets in when we let anything other than God be our reason for rejoicing. Education is no reason to rejoice. Might and fame are not reasons to rejoice. Money is no reason to rejoice. God is greater than all these *things*!

God desires a people who will focus on Him and learn Him. We must learn to rejoice if for no other reason than that God has shown favor to us. Take a moment and rejoice because you know Jesus! Thank you, Lord! Let us stop taking God for granted. He is far more worthy than we think He is.

Now listen to me; I am not mocking anyone or anything. Having education and security in life are honorable things, but they are not to be our reason for living. Our reason for living is to glorify God and serve others with His love. If we pursue the Lord as diligently as we chase our business goals, we would find the Lord prospering our hands more! Maybe not in the ways we want, but we will be equipped in ways we never imagined.

Many ladies feel they need a man to be happy: Christ is better than any man! He will give you the greatest pleasure this world cannot offer.

Be defined by nothing but Christ. Don't be labeled by wealth, fame, or influence. No matter what state you are in: happy, sad, rich, poor, sick or well, focus *only* on the Love of God.

Do everything as unto the Lord! In pleasing the Lord, you will find joy, peace, and satisfaction.

So, if things are not going well, don't take your life! Give it to God! He will show you His loving kindness and turn things around. That is what God delights in.

Reflections for Faith Focus # 18

1. Life is a 'what' from God?

2. When does pride set in?

3. What are our reasons for living?

4. Take a moment and write what this Faith Focus means to you:

_____

_____

_____

_____

_____.

FAITH FOCUS #19

Why God gave us the Bible

2 Tim. 3:15-17 (KJV)

And that from a child thou hast known the holy scriptures, which are able to make thee wise unto salvation through faith which is in Christ Jesus. [16] All scripture is given by inspiration of God, and is profitable for doctrine, for reproof, for correction, for instruction in righteousness: [17] That the man of God may be perfect, thoroughly furnished unto all good works.

As a parent, I give my son responsibilities. It helps him grow into maturity. Often times, I make a list of chores and instructions for him to follow. If he does what is assigned, I reward him. If he does not, he is punished. One of the ways I prepare my son for life is to provide him with instructions and chores. However, there is one thing I can assure you of - I never give him a list of instructions just for his own reading pleasure.

My mother used to leave lists for me. I was supposed to have all the items on the lists completed by the time she returned home from work. Most days I did. But, there were a few times, for whatever reason, I failed to meet her expectations. I am certain you can figure out the rest.

God is the same way. He has provided us with a beautiful set of chores and instructions. We refer to this expansive list as "The Bible."

Unfortunately, many of us have taken the Bible for a mere book of anecdotes and fine quotes. Some believe it is good reading for those dark lonely nights when one feels down. The truth, though, is that The Bible is God's way of producing responsibility and maturity in us. All 66 books of the Bible, as stated in the above verses, are designed to make our lives prosperous through rich guidance and direction.

Tragically, some think the Bible is optional. In the same way in which my mother's list was not optional, how much more so are God's list of chores and instructions not optional for us?

Please, my dearest friends' do not treat the Bible like it is a buffet: there is no picking and choosing what you want. It **ALL** came from God, and it is **ALL** beneficial for our good.

We have all heard or seen the acronym B.I.B.L.E: Basic Instructions Before Leaving Earth!

John 14:15 (KJV)
If ye love me, keep my commandments.

Friends', following God is not always easy. But, if we do, He will strengthen us to do His Will. Be blessed today as you surrender to the Lord!

Reflections for Faith Focus # 19

1. The Bible is God's way of producing what in us?

2. Take a moment and write what this Faith Focus means to you:

_____

_____

_____

_____

_____

_____.

FAITH FOCUS #20

Here's a 13 for You

Proverbs 13:13 (KJV)
Whoso despiseth the word shall be destroyed: but he that feareth the commandment shall be rewarded.

Friday the 13th is a day, in the eyes of many, considered to be unlucky. I, on the other hand, have always been taught that "luck" is not real. Luck is a deception. It binds people to whimsical concepts that have no basis or foundation. Nothing simply *happens*. There is a direct cause for all things - a seed which produces a distinct fruit.

Many people buy into the lie that they have "bad luck." The truth is that they have accepted the deception. If you obey God's Word, you will sow seeds of change, transformation, blessing, and peace. If you ignore the principles of the Bible, you can be certain that destruction lurks at your door.

Galatians 6:7-9 (KJV)
Be not deceived; God is not mocked: for whatsoever a man soweth, that shall he also reap. [8] For he that soweth to his flesh shall of the flesh reap corruption; but he that soweth to the Spirit shall of the Spirit reap life everlasting. [9] And let us not be weary in well doing: for in due season we shall reap, if we faint not.

Your life is a direct result of seeds sown into you. Words, actions, and beliefs, are all seeds which have contributed to your life thus far. If things are not the way God wants them, they can be; just change the seeds you sow. Change the people you relate with. Change the way you think. Ignore the negative people and bad news.

Now, know this: once you start trusting in and respecting the Word of God, things may become difficult. But, if you stick with it, God will reveal His truth in your life.

Luck is irrelevant. God's Word overrules all curses and bad trends. Believe the Bible. Study and meditate on It day and night. Relieve yourself from fear and realize that God rewards everyone who respects His Word!

Reflections for Faith Focus # 20

1. Take a moment and write what this Faith Focus means to you:

_____

_____

_____

_____

_____

_____

_____.

FAITH FOCUS #21

Lessons from Enoch

Hebrews 11:6 (KJV)
But without faith it is impossible to please Him: for he that cometh to God must believe that He is, and that He is a rewarder of them that diligently seek Him.

Ahh... Yes! The fine art of pleasing God can be tricky, especially if you forget the key element: faith!

Indeed, without faith, God cannot be pleased. There are those, however, who are convinced otherwise. But friends, I know that you are not so foolish as to think that God is pleased by any other means. He cannot be pleased without faith!

Hebrews 11:5 (KJV)
By faith Enoch was translated that he should not see death; and was not found, because God had translated him: for before his translation he had this testimony, that he pleased God.

Let us take a lesson from Enoch. Not much is spoken about him throughout the Bible. But, what is written about him is extremely powerful. In the above verse, we learn that before Enoch left this earth, he pleased God. Now that is a bold statement! How many of us can confidently stand and declare that God is totally pleased with us? Enoch can. Let us see how.

Genesis 5:24 (KJV)
And Enoch walked with God: and he was not; for God took him.

Enoch did not die; God took Him. Hebrews says that he *pleased* God. Genesis says that God took Him. We can conclude then that Enoch pleased God so much that God had to have him in Heaven. Enoch walked with God for 300 years. It took him 300 years, but he walked with God by faith. Without faith, God cannot be pleased. From Enoch's life, we learn that God was indeed pleased with Enoch.

Take note of the phrase from Genesis 5, *and he was not.*

Enoch walked out of the natural right into the spirit. Though it took him 300 years, with every step through those three centuries, he became more and more like God and less like himself. He ceased being a fearful, negative, disobedient man. He literally became a man who clearly demonstrated faith and Godly character. God was pleased by his persistent walk of faith.

So, be encouraged! Let patience work in your life. Keep going and don't give up. Learn from every mistake and improve upon every success. It may have taken Enoch 300 years, but he didn't have the Holy Spirit living inside him; *you do.* Trust in the Holy Spirit. He will lead you into a lifestyle that pleases God if you obey Him.

Reflections for Faith Focus # 21

1. Why didn't Enoch die?

2. What does the phrase "and he was not" mean?

3. What is the key element of pleasing God?

4. Take a moment and write what this Faith Focus means to you:

_____

_____

_____

_____

_____.

FAITH FOCUS #22

No More Snackin'!

2 Tim. 2:15 (KJV)

Study to shew thyself approved unto God, a workman that needeth not to be ashamed, rightly dividing the word of truth.

One day, I was in the midst of a fantastic conversation with a good friend of mine. We were working on a special men's project that was to take place during that time frame. As we talked, a thought occurred to me: if reading the Bible is a snack and studying the Bible is a well-balanced meal, how many meals does a person actually eat each day, or even, each week?

Most of us don't go for long without eating; some of us indulge a bit more than others. Just as our stomachs yearn for natural nourishment, our spirits yearn for spiritual nourishment.

As delicious as it might sound, a juicy grilled steak with steamy vegetables soaked in butter, a loaded baked potato, and tall glass of grape, (oh, excuse me,) purple Kool-aide will do nothing for our spirits. Now, if my mother is reading this, (and I know you are) substitute a big tray of lightly steamed broccoli and spaghetti squash - she is holy! However, even that, as healthy as it is, does absolutely nothing for our soul and spirit.

1 Cor. 15:46 (KJV)

Howbeit that was not first which is spiritual, but that which is natural; and afterward that which is spiritual.

Jesus showed us the art of revealing spiritual truth by pointing to natural things we all can relate to. Most people run through each day snacking; they grab something quick at

Starbucks or the gas station. Drive-through restaurants are packed because our lives are too busy for us to prepare a proper meal and sit down to eat it. As a result, health issues are on the rise and our human bodies suffer.

This being the case, how much more do our spirits and souls suffer when we limit our spiritual life to just Sunday service and maybe a mid-week Bible study? Some of us have a short daily devotional; this is a snack. Because we are not feeding our inner selves with the food God provided us with -- The Bible -- we lack strength, focus, and courage to endure the pressures of this life.

Reading can be as simple as glancing through a page of writing or looking at a street sign. Study, however, is an in-depth and time-consuming process of searching out the full meaning of a thing. This is called ***getting an understanding.*** Proverbs 4:7 instructs us to get an understanding of everything the Bible says.

Because there is always something more pressing, many of us won't take the time for a full meal. We end up grabbing a quick snack to kill the hunger pangs. We are killing ourselves! Conversely, running in church late to hear a quick sermon, or glancing at a scripture or two is mere snacking.

Friends, take the time to prepare a full spiritual meal. Set aside some quality time to thoroughly search the meaning of the Bible. Attend the set worship and study times at your church. Clear out three distinct, uninterrupted prayer and study times each day. Yes, you can do this very easily!

If we can find time to watch our favorite TV shows, we can just as easily find three 30-minute segments in our day to study the Bible. Our spirits need it. If we will start doing this, we will notice a verifiable change in our day.

So, stop snacking so much! The Bible is far too important for that. Set aside some time for a good meal. If it wasn't important, Jesus would not have asked God for a daily meal in the Lord's Prayer: *give us this day our daily bread.*

This referred to the manna that fell in the days of Moses. The manna was an entire day's worth of food that fell fresh every day. There were no leftovers either.

Each day God has a special meal prepared just for you. Go get it!

Reflections for Faith Focus # 22

1. What is the difference between a meal and a snack?

2. Study is also called getting what?

3. How can you go about preparing a full spiritual meal?

4. Take a moment and write what this Faith Focus means to you:

_____

_____

_____

_____

_____.

FAITH FOCUS #23

The Prayer Challenge

1 Tim. 2:8 (KJV)

I will therefore that men pray everywhere, lifting up holy hands, without wrath and doubting.

Yesterday morning, as I pulled into the parking lot at my office, I had an overwhelming urge to pray. Now, I like to pray just as much as you. This time, however, I was compelled with a need to pray that seemed to possess me.

I called several people I knew because I wanted them to come by the church and pray with me; no one was available. So, I went to my office and began praying. I had a schedule for the day, but I laid it aside to pursue the Lord.

After a while, one of my covenant brothers called. He said he would meet me at my office. I then called another friend to meet me as well. Within 20 minutes, we were all assembled. We grasped hands and prayed there in the church sanctuary. Oh, how the glory of God filled our hearts!

I was overjoyed because all I wanted to do was thank God and encourage my brothers in the Lord. After praying, we just laughed and encouraged each other. It was such a refreshing time.

Luke 18:1 (KJV)

And he spake a parable unto them to this end, that men ought always to pray, and not to faint;

Brothers and sisters, prayer is such an important part of our lives. Unfortunately, we don't do enough of it. Even in church, prayer is scarce. I could have ignored my urge to pray, but, thank God, I didn't. As a result, others were uplifted and strengthened.

Here is my challenge to you: find at least one other person to pray with every week. Don't whine or beg God for stuff, and don't ask for anything for yourself. Pray together giving God a lot of appreciation and thanks; ask the Lord to strengthen your friend. Let your friend pray for you, and you pray for him or her. You will be so blessed by this.

James 5:16 (KJV)
Confess your faults one to another, and pray one for another, that ye may be healed. The effectual fervent prayer of a righteous man availeth much.

Saints, praying is actually effective: you just have to do it. Many of us do not want to invest the time and patience necessary to pray; however, we **must** do it. If you don't know how to pray well, find your Pastor and ask him or her to teach you how to pray. That is what Jesus' disciples did: they asked the Lord to teach them to pray.

As we gather to pray for each other, we are healed. You will be so blessed! If you already do this, keep it up and encourage others to get involved. Be blessed, and let me know how this changes your life and the lives of others.

Reflections for Faith Focus # 23

1. Why shouldn't we ignore our urge to pray?

2. Who can you find to pray with on a weekly basis?

3. What time every week will you sacrifice to pray?

4. Take a moment and write what this Faith Focus means to you:

_____

_____

_____

_____

_____.

FAITH FOCUS #24

Uniting A House Divided

Matthew 12:25 (KJV)

And Jesus knew their thoughts, and said unto them, Every kingdom divided against itself is brought to desolation; and every city or house divided against itself shall not stand:

Have you ever noticed how divided Christian people are? Everybody thinks they are right and everybody else is wrong. What foolishness!

Pentecostals. Church of God. Baptists. Methodists. Evangelicals. Etc... You name it and there is a group to fit your preference: a veritable smorgasbord of spiritual experiences.

If you like noise, there is a church for you. If you like quiet, there is a church for you. If you want to roll on the floor, there is a church for you. If you want to be done in 45 minutes, there is a church for you.

It seems as though everybody can get what they want out of church except God! God wants sinners saved. However, He can't get what He wants because everybody is too divided.

Blacks hate the way whites worship. Whites say blacks preach too loud. Americans say Africans pray too long. And if that is not enough, nobody believes the same thing!

I am still amazed that so many Christian denominations have spawned from the same Bible. Only in Christendom are people allowed to render various interpretations of scripture. You can't do that with Shakespeare! When you read his grand literary works, there is only one acceptable interpretation. In the church, though, we believe what we want and do as we please.

If you ever read the Book of Acts, and I challenge you to do it today, you will see that the Church was united! There were churches in different places and cities, but they all functioned as one. Today this is not so.

There can be two churches on adjacent corners, from the same denomination, and they won't fellowship together. Pastors are trying to steal each others' members, and all the while the neighborhood they are located in is going to hell. God is not pleased!

One day we will realize that we all have a common faith in Jesus Christ. We will realize that our distinct differences are strengths which, if embraced and appreciated, will enable us to reach a broader more diverse group of people for Christ.

One day we will realize that our main job, as Christians, is to lead people to Jesus, and that we cannot do this alone. No one man can do it. No single church or denomination can do it alone. Only the united Body of Christ can do it. Only together can we fulfill the will of God and bring pleasure to the Lord and peace to mankind.

You may not like the President, but he is right about change. Not necessarily political change, but there is definitely a spiritual renewal happening right now. Churches are waking up and working together. They are crossing denominational, social, racial, and generational lines in order to do the work of ministry the right way.

My brothers and sisters, by the direction of the Holy Ghost, there are established and soon-to-be-established ministries linked together to help each other fulfill the will of God. These ministries exist to change the dynamics of church and ministry by breaking from tradition to restore integrity and excellence to the House of the Lord!

Pray for these organizations. Join them. God is calling His people to move with Him. In these last days, the Lord is more aggressive concerning bringing unity to His House. He desires that His House stand strong and be a refuge of hope in this dark world.

Rejoice, my friends! The Lord is restoring honor to His House!

Reflections for Faith Focus # 24

1. God wants who to be saved?

2. What have you learned from your reading of the Book of Acts?

3. Our distinct differences are strengths which need to be what?

4. Take a moment and write what this Faith Focus means to you:

_____

_____

_____

_____

_____.

FAITH FOCUS #25

What are YOU Watching?

Matthew 26:40-41 (KJV)

And he cometh unto the disciples, and findeth them asleep, and saith unto Peter, What, could ye not watch with Me one hour? [41] Watch and pray, that ye enter not into temptation: the spirit indeed is willing, but the flesh is weak.

Gregoreuo: Greek 1127, Strong's: gregoreuo, gray-gor-yoo'-o; from Greek 1453 (egeiro); to keep awake, i.e. watch (literal or figurative) :- be vigilant, wake, (be) watch (-ful).

Friends, take a look at the word "watch." It means to keep awake and be vigilant. Jesus was saddened: His disciples were not alert, they were asleep! Unfortunately, not much has changed among His disciples over 2000 years; many of us are **still** sleep.

Now, we are highly conscientious concerning church activity: Choir Jamborees, Women's Day, Usher Appreciation Day, and so forth. However, we are not equally alert and watchful when it comes to other matters of the Kingdom: we are asleep to the Will of God.

Yes, this is a strong assertion, but Jesus tells us very clearly that temptation is on the prowl. Therefore, we must be very watchful. We cannot afford to be asleep!

The Lord reveals how we are supposed to watch: through prayer. He said to watch and pray to avoid temptation. Temptation is all around us. It seeks to distract us and lull us to sleep causing us to become ineffective and useless to God. Temptation causes us to focus on ourselves and desensitizes us to the needs of others.

Watching allows us to recognize temptation while prayer gives us the power to overcome and defeat it. Our spirits really do want to please the Lord. Unfortunately, our flesh only wants to please itself.

For example, when it is time to fast, our spirit actually *wants* to seek God. However, our flesh wants to run to the vending machine every 5 minutes. Why? Because the flesh is weak and wants to do what is easy.

Granted, it *is* hard to deny oneself the pleasure of eating in order to draw closer to God. Conversely, though, it is equally as easy to stuff our faces and offer the age-old defense that, *God knows my heart.*

The sad part is that, when we are not fasting, we can, and often will, go the entire day without eating because we are too busy and don't have time to stop for a break. But during fasting, all we can think about is how "hongree" we are. That, my dear friends, is a perfect example of being asleep.

So, we pray to strengthen ourselves and to keep ourselves focused. In essence, prayer is what disciplines us in spiritual obedience. Jesus is looking for His disciples to watch and pray. Not just on Sunday, but all throughout each and every day. Be prayerful and alert! Only by this can we be true representatives of Christ.

God is waiting to do so much in our lives. However, it only flows through the channel of prayer; it is just that simple! So, let us break the fleshly habits in our lives through watchful prayer!

Reflections for Faith Focus # 25

1. What does the word "watch" mean?

2. What does watching allow you to recognize?

3. What does prayer do?

4. Take a moment and write what this Faith Focus means to you:

_____

_____

_____

_____

_____.

FAITH FOCUS #26

Dealing with Pressure

Luke 22:41-46 (KJV)

And He was withdrawn from them about a stone's cast, and kneeled down, and prayed, [42] Saying, Father, if Thou be willing, remove this cup from Me: nevertheless not My will, but Thine, be done. [43] And there appeared an angel unto Him from heaven, strengthening Him. [44] And being in an agony He prayed more earnestly: and His sweat was as it were great drops of blood falling down to the ground. [45] And when He rose up from prayer, and was come to His disciples, He found them sleeping for sorrow, [46] And said unto them, Why sleep ye? rise and pray, lest ye enter into temptation.

Most of us face pressure all the time. Thankfully, the Bible instructs us by providing clear examples on how we are to deal with pressure. Jesus is our role model: He had stress and pressure, too.

In the above passage, we are provided a glimpse into the life of our Lord. Jesus was under a great deal of stress: one of His best friends had just betrayed Him and sold Him out; He was about to die and had to do it willingly; His other friends left Him on a cliff alone. He was in much agony! I am certain we can all relate to some of those issues. However, the question is, how did Jesus handle it? Easy: He prayed!

Now, I realize that this seems too simple for many of you. But, think about this: if I were to tell you to go on a quest - travel to South America; find the passage of tranquility hidden deep in the Amazon; ask an old wise man for a blue rose - all your worries will cease. Why? Because you would perceive that you had something concrete to do and to hold onto.

Of course, many of you may not do that at all. Tragically, in many of our hearts, we attach our peace to something natural. Human beings like stuff like that- going on a quest! It is fun and adventurous!

Prayer, on the other hand, is often boring and uneventful compared to a quest. Indeed, it may be that way at first, but it is the avenue God has chosen to usher His Will and promises into our lives.

Prayer does not change God's mind! When we pray, many of us actually try to change God's mind: we want **Him** to submit to **our** will! God ignores such prayers.

Jesus prayed and things got worse. When agony struck Him, He prayed more earnestly. Many of us stop praying if things don't get better. Not the Lord! He prayed more! As we saw in the above passage, an angel brought Him strength. Strength comes through prayer - not the club.

It takes humility to pray. Many of us are too proud to pray. If we are high-minded or intellectual, we tend to think we can outwit our enemy and figure things out on our own. Friends, this is pride! Yes, God gifted us with strategic minds. But, that gift **must be** submitted to Christ; God has to show us how to use it. That comes through prayer. Unfortunately, our lack of prayer causes our stressful pressure to morph into agony.

James 5:13 (KJV)
Is any among you afflicted? let him pray.

The solution to all things comes through prayer. If you choose not to pray, you will fall asleep. When life has a choke hold on you, if you do not pray, you will faint under the pressure.

Being asleep does not mean being asleep in the normal sense of the word. Depression is a form of being asleep. Fear can cause a person to fall asleep. Drinking away your sorrows will cause you to fall asleep. Having a bad attitude puts a person in the sleep zone. Not praying or reading the Bible causes a person to fall asleep.

Anything that is not part of God's will is sleep. The pressures of life come to put us in a stupor to render us helpless and useless to God – in other words, it comes to put us to sleep!

Jesus told His disciples to pray that they would not fall prey to temptation. They were all under stress. Jesus, though, chose to pray through the struggle. As a result, He found strength from Heaven. He still had to do the Will of God, but He was provided with the strength He needed to carry out His task.

His disciples, in contrast, (Luke 22:45) were overwhelmed with sorrow. Unlike their Lord, they allowed their sorrow to get the best of them. He prayed while they slept. Unfortunately, they awoke to find that they had disappointed the Lord.

Saints, don't fall asleep! Start praying more than you have before. If you only pray 2 minutes per day, increase that to 4 minutes. If you only pray 2 times per day, pray 3 times. Pray about everything and let God bless you.

Reflections for Faith Focus # 26

1. What did Jesus do to deal with pressure?

2. A lack of prayer does what to pressure?

3. List examples of being sleep?

4. Take a moment and write what this Faith Focus means to you:

_____

_____

_____

_____

_____.

FAITH FOCUS #27

Just Know That You WIN!

Isaiah 46:9-10 (KJV)

Remember the former things of old: for I am God, and there is none else; I am God, and there is none like Me, [10] Declaring the end from the beginning, and from ancient times the things that are not yet done, saying, My counsel shall stand, and I will do all My pleasure:

Have you ever noticed how crazy God talks?

He will tell a person to go into business when he or she is broke and bankrupt.

He says, **What a beautiful day it is!** when the rain is pouring.

He chooses ill-equipped and unprepared people to be His representatives.

He tells us, **Walk with Me! ...**But never tells us where we are going!

Somehow God just expects us to drop everything and put Him first. That is crazy!

Let me remind you, though, that God does not think like we think. His vantage point is far better than ours: He sees in reverse. He knows every outcome, so His news is always good news! When He comes to us, He is not surprised. No matter how hard things are right now, God knows that we will rise above.

As dark as this world is, God has already seen its salvation and the destruction of evil. If we trust Him, then it behooves us to walk by faith and rejoice!

If you are on a basketball team, (you all know how much I love basketball,) and you already know that your team is going to win the game, you can release stress and play pressure-free because you already know the outcome: you win! The game might be close - your team may even be down by a large deficit at times - but even that is irrelevant. You know the outcome!

Our problem, though, is we want to blow our opponent out of the water: we want to win by 50 points! We want the game to be easy - no challenge. That is not how it goes. There are some things we face that will take us to the brink of our ability: our education cannot help us; our experiences cannot help us; it will be all we can do just to lift our hand and say, *Thank you, Lord.*

But even then, we have a place to celebrate because...We Win! Whether we win by 100 points or 1 point, we still win.

I say this because I have learned that, without a doubt, God already has the solution before the problem presents itself.

At one point, I had to stand more fervently than I ever had before. I was broken, to the point of tears and was about to throw in the towel. But then, out of the belly of my despair, I began to sing songs of praise to the Lord. At that exact moment, my strength was restored. I discovered that I could stand a while longer trusting God to meet this great need.

Little did I know, though, that, while I was still hoping He would come through, God already had waiting for me what I needed. Within minutes, all was handled and God received all the glory!

My point is this: God will not tell us to do anything that He does not already have the solution for. Everything we need is already in place! Hold on and don't give up! He has seen the outcome. He has given us His Spirit to strengthen and guide us to that glorious end result. We may have to cry and suffer loss, but keep trusting God. Our journey may be long and difficult, but remember: WE WIN!

So, remind yourself to see things from God's perspective: you have already won. Keep your eyes on this truth: no matter what you face, the Lord has the Winner's Circle waiting for you. Just keep going!

Reflections for Faith Focus # 27

1. What crazy things has God told you to do?

2. If we trust God, then what should we do?

3. How can we adjust our minds to see our situations the way God does?

4. Take a moment and write what this Faith Focus means to you:

_____

_____

_____

_____

_____.

FAITH FOCUS, VOLUME I

FAITH FOCUS #28

You are Not Dead!

James 1:2-4 (KJV)
My brethren, count it all joy when ye fall into divers temptations; [3] Knowing this, that the trying of your faith worketh patience. [4] But let patience have her perfect work, that ye may be perfect and entire, wanting nothing.

I recently got a chance to sit with a man whom I consider to be my greatest mentor. Many years ago, this man poured his life into me. He taught me how to pray, study the bible, witness, and be bold for Jesus! Just thinking of those days so long ago puts a smile on my face. I wanted to cry then, but I am grateful now.

Yes, he was rough on me at times, but it made me stronger. Because this man aggressively instilled Christ in my heart, I am able to endure much as I fulfill the Will of God for my life.

I would venture to say that one of the main reasons so many Christians are so weak and fickle today is because they were never truly mentored and held accountable. Therefore, when someone corrects them or speaks too rough to them, they break down and leave the church or run away. And if the devil were to confront them, they would cower before him as though God is dead. I digress.

My mentor still amazes me. I spent two days with him, and he sparked something powerful in me. He has faced great tragedy and pain, but you would never know it. He is bolder now than ever before!

You see, the devil tried to kill him. He shared with me how God showed him a dream just before all hell broke loose against him. In the dream, (I am paraphrasing,) he stood on a street corner with many people. Some men came with machine guns and began shooting everyone. Bodies falling everywhere, my mentor fell down with the other bodies and played dead.

Suddenly, police sirens sounded and the killers ran away. As they left, my mentor lifted himself from the ground. One of the killers turned. Seeing him still alive, the killer shouted to his friends as they ran off, "He Ain't Dead!"

Saints, I won't go into all that my mentor has suffered and endured. The bottom line is that, with all that occurred, Satan meant his demise. But He ain't dead! You can apply that to your own life. You Ain't Dead!

We spend so much time complaining about what isn't right and what we don't have that we miss the miracle that surrounds us every day: Life!

You Ain't Dead! Keep believing! Hold on to the promise of God. You may need to go through a time of recovery, but never lose sight of the fact that God has preserved your life. That is a Great Miracle. Rejoice in that and allow God to usher you into a greater glory!

Reflections for Faith Focus # 28

1. Take a moment and write what this Faith Focus means to you:

_____

_____

_____

_____

_____

_____

_____

_____.

FAITH FOCUS #29

By-Products of Faith!

<u>James 1:3 (KJV)</u>
Knowing this, that the trying of your faith worketh patience.

Patience is the bi-product of tried faith. As we wait on God and endure hardness, patience is erected. This process is hardly ever fun and exciting. In fact, in many cases, it can be downright, disgustingly excruciating. Oh, but when the storm is over and the tide subsides, as Bishop Clyde Nichols would say - ***Great Joy!***

You see, this process is a most essential part of our development as spiritual beings. The discipline necessary to discern when to act and what to do requires patience. Dealing with God requires patience - much more than most of us would like to admit.

God moves in ways unknown to the majority of our senses. To keep us on course, God speaks to us. Our senses get bombarded and overwhelmed with fears, failures, and experiences. To override those things, God shares His Will through His Word to keep us on course.

A map is true in good or bad weather. If you follow, even through bad weather, you will reach your destination. However, as you travel, some storms may delay or even detour you. Patience ensures that you arrive safely.

2 Cor. 4:18 (KJV)
While we look not at the things which are seen, but at the things which are not seen: for the things which are seen are temporal; but the things which are not seen are eternal.

Patience outlasts opposition!

Therefore, we focus on Christ and not on anything else. No matter what is against us, we *can* outlast it. We *will* reach our destination with safety. The road may be rough and the ride may get bumpy. But, the patience which has been constructed in our lives will propel us to God's unlimited favor.

So, take some risks! Allow your faith to be challenged. There can only be one outcome: Patience!

Reflections for Faith Focus # 29

1. How is patience produced?

2. The discipline to discern requires what?

3. Patience will propel you where?

4. Take a moment and write what this Faith Focus means to you:

_____

_____

_____

_____

_____.

FAITH FOCUS #30

Live and have Peace

<u>Jeremiah 29:4-7 (KJV)</u>

Thus saith the Lord of hosts, the God of Israel, unto all that are carried away captives, whom I have caused to be carried away from Jerusalem unto Babylon; [5] Build ye houses, and dwell in them; and plant gardens, and eat the fruit of them; [6] Take ye wives, and beget sons and daughters; and take wives for your sons, and give your daughters to husbands, that they may bear sons and daughters; that ye may be increased there, and not diminished. [7] And seek the peace of the city whither I have caused you to be carried away captives, and pray unto the Lord for it: for in the peace thereof shall ye have peace.

The Prophet Jeremiah did not have an easy task. He had to tell the people of God the *Ugly Truth!* There were many people who lied in the name of the Lord, and, wouldn't you know it, a lot of people really wanted to hear those lies. They hated and mistreated Jeremiah because he said hard things. People today, like then, want to be told cute things. If they don't hear what they want, they turn on the preacher and get mad with God.

God, however, is not confronted by our immaturity. He remains steadfast in His efforts of calling His people to responsibility and growth. We must stop looking at God like it is His job to save us all the time. We need to recognize that He, through Christ, has already given us the *Power to Triumph Victoriously!*

In the above passage - and do feel free to read the entire 29th Chapter for yourself; it will bless you - Jeremiah has to adjust the mindset of a people in bondage, in captivity. They are suffering and hurt. Many of them are upset and frustrated because their situation keeps getting worse. They are oppressed and have no peace. They have called on the Lord, and God is seemingly nowhere. When He does finally speak to them, it is not what they had in mind: they wanted God to rush in and fix everything.

There are some people around you right now who cannot praise God unless things are wonderful. If the temperature is a tad too hot, they are depressed. They only smile on payday. They worry about everything and are fearful to make decisions. When God speaks, they are often still sad because He places the responsibility on them.

Yes! God may be Superman, but you are Batman. You have a utility belt! Use the **faith** God gave you to start solving your own problems. The Power of Christ, which God equipped you with, resides within you. Don't run off and put Long Island in your Iced Tea to drown your sorrows; **go slap the devil!**

Alright, settle down so I can finish. Jeremiah encourages the captives to stop waiting on God to get them out of their problems and start living! That's right, family; *start living!*

Through Jeremiah, God told the captives to: build houses, own land, get married, and raise your family! Then He told them to seek peace for their government. Yes, He did!

We must pray and sow peace into the very people and environment which oppresses us. Only then will we find peace for ourselves. Why? Because whatever we sow is what we reap.

John 10:10 (KJV)
The thief cometh not, but for to steal, and to kill, and to destroy: I am come that they might have life, and that they might have it more abundantly.

Live today! Jesus came for us to live. Stop complaining and live. If you don't like your job, find a new one. If you need a house, go and get one. Start businesses. Stop complaining about your husband and celebrate him.

Follow the Holy Spirit: He will lead you into living. Pray for peace in your neighborhood and city. Pray for your boss and company. Pray for God to bring peace to those who hurt you. The scripture said,...*for in the peace thereof shall ye have peace.*

God wants to turn our "Barren Land" into our "Promised Land." He wants everyone around us to see the splendor of His grace and glory through our lives. His plan is to put us on display right in the midst of our mess!

Smile now and start living! Go do what God placed in your heart. Stop standing still afraid to make choices. Whatever you choose, God will back you. You have the keys to His Kingdom; you can't fail! Whatever you apply your hands to do shall succeed.

Live now and sow peace. You don't have time to be sad. It is God's Will that you live. And, as you live and sow peace, God will be glorified; your deliverance **will** find you.

Whooooooooooooo! You should just shout **Hallelujah** right now!

Family, like Jeremiah, I came to give you the **Ugly Truth.** God is giving you instruction. Everything may not be as you like it, but keep walking in God and be faithful to Him. Before long, He will make all things fresh and new. Don't, however, be sad and weary until He moves.

Just Live!

Just Live!

Just Live!

And **Have Peace!**

God will never forsake His Promise. That means YOU!

Reflections for Faith Focus # 30

1. Have you ever been angry with God for telling you something you didn't want to hear? Explain.

2. How does Batman relate to you?

3. What things can you do to live?

4. Take a moment and write what this Faith Focus means to you:

_____

_____

_____

_____

_____.

NOTES:

ABOUT THE AUTHOR

Adrian Taylor, Jr. mentors hundreds of young people through the S.U.C.C.E.S.S & "The Setup" Campus Outreach Programs. These programs primarily focus college students on the greater principles of Christ. While attending college himself, Adrian asked the Lord why so many people were unsuccessful in college. The answer was found in Joshua, Chapter 1, Verse 8:

This book of the law shall not depart out of thy mouth: but thou shalt meditate therein day and night, that thou mayest observe to do according to all that is written therein: for then thou shalt make thy way prosperous, and then thou shalt have good success.

Adrian developed a regular gathering to teach the principles of the Bible to his fellow students. That initial gathering in the late 90's spawned what has now become a major campus take-over for Christ. Students throughout Southeast Missouri are finding purpose, direction, and healing for their lives.

"They are the next generation of politicians, business leaders, and educators, and we **must** *take the time to direct them in ways of righteousness so God can be honored,"* Taylor says emphatically.

Countless young people have been impacted by the life and ministry of Adrian Taylor, Jr. He has seen the most severely depressed as well as the most academically challenged find freedom from their limitations. These young people are now able to walk in the liberty and peace which can only be found through faith in Jesus Christ. Taylor's philosophy is that academic and spiritual success are synonymous; only through following Christ can one achieve both while pleasing God at the same time.

www.ingramcontent.com/pod-product-compliance
Lightning Source LLC
Chambersburg PA
CBHW052126090426
42741CB00009B/1972